THE SECRET AND POWER OF SELF-BELIEF

OVERCOMING LIFE CHALLENGES WITH CONFIDENCE

DR. JAGADEESH PILLAI

|| Dedicated to all wisdom seekers around the World ||

Contents

Prayer   *vii*

About The Author   *ix*

Preface   *xiii*

1. Understanding The Secret And Power Of Self-belief 1
   And Its Impact On Overcoming Challenges

Part 1

2. Identifying And Challenging Negative Self-talk   5

Part 2

3. Setting Realistic Goals And Prioritizing Self-care   9

Part 3

4. The Power Of Gratitude And Mindfulness   13

Part 4

5. Building Resilience And Coping With Setbacks   17

Part 5

6. Building Confidence Through Positive Habits   23

Part 6

7. Overcoming Fear Of Failure And Rejection   29

Part 7

8. Managing Emotions The Importance Of Self-care   33

Part 8

9. Understanding And Managing Self-criticism   37

Part 9

10. Developing A Growth Mindset   43

Part 10

Contents

11. Building Support Systems And Connecting With   47

     Others

Part 11

12. Finding And Pursuing Your Passions   51

Part 12

13. Understanding And Managing Perfectionism   55

Part 13

14. Building Self-compassion   61

Part 14

15. Overcoming Life Challenges With Confidence In   65

     Self-belief

Part 15

Other Books Of The Author   69

Contact   77

Prayer

**"Om Bhadram Karnebhih Shrunuyaama
DevaahBhadram Pashyemaakshabhiryajatraah
SthirairangaistushtuvaamsastanoobhihVyashema
Devahitam YadaayuhSwasti Na Indro
VridhashravaahSwasti Nah Pooshaa
VishwavedaahSwasti Nastaarkshyo ArishtanemihSwasti
No Brihaspatir DadhaatuOm Shantih, Shantih, Shantih"**

The literal meaning of this mantra is: OM. O Gods! Let us hear auspicious words from our ears. O reverent Gods! Let us behold propitious visions from our eyes, let our organs and body be stable, healthy, and strong. Let us do that which is pleasing to the gods in the life span allotted to us. May Indra, inscribed in the scriptures, bring us fortune! May Pushan, the knower of the world, grant us prosperity! May Trakshya, who vanquishes enemies, bestow us with blessings! May Brihaspati bring us success!
OM Peace, Peace, Peace.

About The Author

Dr. Jagadeesh Pillai is a renowned Guinness World Record holder, writer, and researcher hailing from Varanasi, also known as the abode of Lord Shiva. With a Ph.D. in Vedic Science and a range of creative ideas and achievements, he is a true polymath. He is the author of more than 100 books including Research Publications. Although his roots can be traced back to Kerala, the people of Varanasi hold him in high regard and affectionately consider him one of their own.

In 1998, Dr. Pillai was offered a job at Banaras Hindu University, but he left the position after only two months to pursue greater goals in life. He believed that in order to study Indian scriptures and engage in other creative endeavours, he needed to retire from the daily grind of working solely for money at a young age.

He started an export business from scratch, using the knowledge he had gained from a previous job in the industry. His intelligence and unique approach to business led to great success in a short period of time, earning him more in just a decade and a half than he would have in a lifetime working in a government job. Upon the passing of Dr. APJ Abdul Kalam, Dr. Pillai decided to leave the business and dedicate himself to reading, studying, researching, and experimenting.

During his tenure in the export business, Dr. Pillai traveled to over 16 countries, gaining valuable insight and experiencing the world and life in detail.

Dr. Pillai has achieved four Guinness World Records in the following subjects:

"Script to Screen" - In this record, Dr. Pillai produced and directed an animation film within the shortest time possible, breaking the previous record set by Canadians. He has also received numerous national and international awards and recognitions for this achievement.

Longest Line of Postcards - For this record, Dr. Pillai created a line of 16,300 postcards on the occasion of the 163rd anniversary of Indian Postal Day. The event also included a questionnaire about the Indian flag.

Largest Poster Awareness Campaign - Dr. Pillai designed an awareness campaign on the subject of "Beti Bachao - Beti Padhao" (Save the Girl Child - Educate the Girl Child) to achieve this record.

Largest Envelope - In tribute to the Indian Prime Minister's "Make in India" initiative, Dr. Pillai created a 4000 square meter envelope using waste paper to achieve this record.

Attempted - **70000 Candles on a 210 kg Cake** - To celebrate the 70th Indian Independence Day, Dr. Pillai attempted to light 70,000 candles on a 210 kg cake, which was recorded in World Records India.

Attempted - **Documentary on Dhamek Stupa of Sarnath in 17 Languages** - Dr. Pillai attempted to create a documentary on the Dhamek Stupa of Sarnath, dubbing it in 17 different languages. The result of this attempt is currently awaiting confirmation from the Guinness World Records.

Dr. Pillai is skilled in teaching the Bhagavad Gita, a Hindu scripture, and is popular among young people. He has helped many young people improve their lives through his motivational teachings.

In addition to teaching, he has composed and sung numerous Sanskrit Bhajans and patriotic songs.

He has also written and directed several short films and documentaries for awareness campaigns, and has volunteered with the police in both UP and Kerala to spread awareness about various issues through videos and photography.

Incredibly, he has produced and directed over 100 documentaries about the city of Varanasi, all on his own.

He has also helped and guided more than 25 boys and girls to achieve world records through creative and innovative methods. He is a multifaceted person who uses his intellect and the blessings given to him by God to excel in various areas. He is both a teacher and a student, always learning and teaching, and is able to master any subject he comes across.

He is a selfless social activist and motivational speaker who has overcome struggles and failures to become a successful and enthusiastic individual with a rich life experience.

In addition to his work with the Bhagavad Gita, he is also an efficient Tarot card reader, Astro-Vastu consultant, and a talented singer and composer. He has sung the entire Ram Charita Manas and Bhagavad Gita in his own compositions, and has sung the phrase "Lokah Samastha Sukhino Bhavantu" in 50 different languages. He is currently working on a detailed and scientific study of Vedas, Upanishads, Puranas, and the Bhagavad Gita. He has also composed and sung the Hanuman Chalisa and Gayatri Mantra in 108 and 1008 different compositions, respectively.

Awards - Four Times Guinness World Records, Winner of Mahatma Gandhi Vishwa Shanti Puraskar, Mahatma Gandhi Global Peace Ambassador, Kashi Ratna Award, Dr. APJ Abdul Kalam Motivational Person of the Year 2017, Mother Teresa Award, Indira Gandhi Priyadarshini Award, Bharat Vikas Ratna Award, Udyog Ratna Award, Vigyan Prasar Award, Poorvanchal Ratn Samman.

PREFACE

Self-belief is one of the most powerful tools we have to help us overcome life's challenges. It is a combination of self-esteem, self-worth, and confidence that can shape our lives and guide us towards success. Without self-belief, it can be easy to fall into negative thought patterns and be held back by fear, doubt, and insecurity. However, when we cultivate self-belief, we open ourselves up to a world of possibilities and become equipped to tackle life's obstacles head-on.

In this book, "The Secret and Power of Self-Belief: Overcoming Life Challenges with Confidence," we will explore the many facets of self-belief and how it can impact our lives. Through practical advice and inspiring stories, we will delve into topics such as managing negative self-talk, setting realistic goals, building resilience, overcoming fear of failure, managing emotions, developing a growth mindset, connecting with others, finding our passions, managing perfectionism, building self-compassion, and cultivating gratitude and mindfulness. We will also explore how to build confidence through positive habits.

To inspire and encourage you on your journey, we've included fifteen unique quotes on the subject of self-belief. May they offer you motivation, encouragement, and hope as you work towards developing and strengthening your own self-belief.

We hope that this book will serve as a roadmap to help you unlock the secret and power of self-belief, overcome life's challenges with confidence, and live a life full of purpose, passion, and joy.

৪১

I

Understanding the Secret and Power of Self-Belief and Its Impact on Overcoming Challenges

Self-belief is a powerful force that can help us overcome life's challenges and achieve our goals. However, many of us struggle with self-doubt and a lack of confidence, which can hold us back from reaching our full potential. In this book, we will explore the secrets and power of self-belief and how it can be harnessed to help us overcome life's obstacles and live a more fulfilling life.

The impact of self-belief on our lives is profound. When we believe in ourselves and our abilities, we are more likely to take risks, pursue our passions, and overcome challenges. On the other hand, when we lack self-belief, we may be more likely to give up when faced with obstacles, or miss out on opportunities because we don't feel confident enough to take action.

Self-belief is not just about feeling confident or optimistic. It is about having a deep-rooted belief in ourselves and our abilities, regardless of the circumstances or obstacles we may face. This type of self-belief can help us overcome challenges and achieve our goals because it provides us with the resilience and determination to persist, even when things are difficult.

In this chapter, we will examine the key elements of self-belief and how they impact our lives. We will also explore the ways in which self-belief can be developed and strengthened over time, and the role that it plays in helping us overcome challenges and live a more fulfilling life.

By understanding the secret and power of self-belief, we can develop the confidence and resilience necessary to overcome life's challenges and achieve our goals. So, let us begin our journey to discover the full potential of this powerful force within us.

*"Believe in yourself and all that you are.
Know that there is something inside you that
is greater than any obstacle."*

- Christian D. Larson

II

Identifying and Challenging Negative Self-Talk

Negative self-talk is a common barrier to developing strong self-belief and confidence. It is the internal dialogue we have with ourselves that undermines our abilities and creates self-doubt. Negative self-talk can take many forms, including self-criticism, comparisons to others, and predictions of failure. It can be subtle, pervasive, and insidious, affecting every aspect of our lives.

The first step in overcoming negative self-talk is to become aware of it. This may require paying close attention to your thoughts and how you talk to yourself. Common forms of negative self-talk include phrases like "I can't do this", "I'm not good enough", or "I'll never succeed". When you notice these types of thoughts, it is important to acknowledge them and understand their impact on your self-belief.

Once you have identified your negative self-talk, it is time to challenge it. This can be done by questioning the evidence for these thoughts, examining your own experiences, and looking for alternative explanations. For example, if you are telling yourself "I can't do this", you might ask yourself, "What evidence do I have to support this thought?" or "What is the worst that can happen if I try and fail?"

Challenging negative self-talk also involves replacing it with positive and empowering thoughts. This can be done by creating affirmations or positive self-statements that counterbalance the negative self-talk. For example, if you are telling yourself "I'm not good enough", you might replace this thought with, "I am capable and competent" or "I have the skills and abilities to succeed".

In addition to challenging negative self-talk, it is also important to develop a growth mindset. This involves seeing challenges as opportunities for growth and learning, rather than as threats to our abilities or self-worth. A growth mindset can help you to be more resilient and optimistic, even in the face of setbacks and obstacles.

Challenging negative self-talk and developing a growth mindset are essential components of building strong self-belief and confidence. By overcoming negative self-talk, you can learn to believe in yourself and your abilities, which will help you to overcome life's challenges and achieve your goals.

"The only limit to our realization of tomorrow will be our doubts of today."

- Franklin D. Roosevelt

III

Setting Realistic Goals and Prioritizing Self-Care

Setting goals and prioritizing self-care are important components of developing strong self-belief and confidence. By setting realistic goals, you can focus your energy and attention on what is important to you, and by prioritizing self-care, you can create the foundation for mental and physical well-being.

When setting goals, it is important to keep them realistic and achievable. This means taking into account your current resources, skills, and experiences, and setting goals that are aligned with your values and priorities. It is also important to break larger goals down into smaller, more manageable steps, and to celebrate each step along the way.

In addition to setting realistic goals, it is also important to develop a growth mindset. This involves seeing challenges as opportunities for growth and learning, rather than as threats to your abilities or self-worth. A growth mindset can help you to be more resilient and optimistic, even in the face of setbacks and obstacles.

Prioritizing self-care is also crucial for developing strong self-belief and confidence. This means taking care of your mental and physical well-being through activities like exercise, mindfulness, and rest. It also means taking care of your emotional well-being by seeking support and connection, and by practicing self-compassion and gratitude.

Self-care is an investment in yourself and your well-being. When you prioritize self-care, you are creating the foundation for a healthy and fulfilling life. It is also a powerful tool for overcoming life's challenges and developing strong self-belief and confidence.

Setting realistic goals and prioritizing self-care are essential components of developing strong self-belief and confidence. By setting goals that are aligned with your values and priorities, and by taking care of your mental and physical well-being, you can create the foundation for a fulfilling and successful life.

"Confidence comes not from always being right but from not fearing to be wrong."

- Peter T. Mcintyre

ଚଚ

IV

The Power of Gratitude and Mindfulness

Gratitude and mindfulness are powerful tools for building self-belief and confidence. When we practice gratitude, we focus on what we are thankful for in our lives, which helps us to shift our attention away from negative thoughts and feelings. Mindfulness involves paying attention to our thoughts, feelings, and sensations in the present moment without judgment, which can help us to become more aware of our negative self-talk and to shift our focus from self-criticism to self-compassion.

Practicing gratitude can help to boost our mood, increase feelings of well-being, and improve our relationships with others. By focusing on what we are thankful for, we are able to appreciate the positive aspects of our lives, which can help us to feel more confident and empowered.

Mindfulness, on the other hand, can help to reduce stress and anxiety by providing a sense of calm and clarity. It can also help us to become more aware of our thoughts and feelings, which can improve our emotional regulation and boost our confidence.

To practice gratitude and mindfulness, it is helpful to set aside time each day to reflect on what we are grateful for and to focus on the present moment. This could involve keeping a gratitude journal, meditating, or simply taking a few moments each day to focus on our breath and become more mindful of our thoughts and feelings.

Another effective strategy is to engage in activities that promote gratitude and mindfulness, such as yoga, tai chi, or walking in nature. These activities can help us to feel more connected to ourselves and the world around us, which can improve our overall sense of well-being and increase our self-confidence.

Gratitude and mindfulness are powerful tools for building self-belief and confidence. By focusing on what we are thankful for and becoming more mindful of our thoughts and feelings, we can reduce stress and anxiety, boost our mood, and improve our emotional regulation, all of which can help us to overcome life's challenges with confidence.

"Believe you can and you're halfway there."

- Theodore Roosevelt

V

Building Resilience and Coping with Setbacks

Building resilience and coping with setbacks are important components of developing strong self-belief and confidence. Resilience is the ability to bounce back from adversity, and it is a critical component of mental and emotional well-being. Coping with setbacks is an essential part of life, and it is important to develop strategies that help you to move through challenges and setbacks with grace and confidence.

To build resilience, it is important to cultivate a growth mindset. This involves seeing challenges as opportunities for growth and learning, rather than as threats to your abilities or self-worth. A growth mindset can help you to be more resilient and optimistic, even in the face of setbacks and obstacles.

In addition to cultivating a growth mindset, there are several other strategies that can help you to build resilience and cope with setbacks. These strategies include:

Practicing self-compassion: Treating yourself with kindness and understanding, rather than self-criticism, can help you to be more resilient and confident.

Building a support network: Surrounding yourself with supportive friends and family can provide you with the encouragement and motivation you need to overcome life's challenges.

Engaging in physical activity: Exercise can help to boost your mood and energy levels, and it can also help you to manage stress and anxiety.

Maintaining a positive outlook: Focusing on the good in your life, and looking for opportunities to see the best in others, can help you to maintain a positive outlook and a confident perspective.

When you experience setbacks, it is important to adopt a proactive approach to coping. This means taking care of your mental and physical well-being, seeking support and connection, and using positive self-talk to help you maintain a confident perspective.

Building resilience and coping with setbacks are essential components of developing strong self-belief and confidence. By cultivating a growth mindset, practicing self-compassion, building a support network, engaging in physical activity, and maintaining a positive outlook, you can develop the resilience and confidence you need to overcome life's challenges and achieve your goals.

"Don't let yesterday take up too much of today."

- Will Rogers

VI

Building Confidence through Positive Habits

Confidence is a key component in overcoming life's challenges, and it can be developed and strengthened through positive habits. Building positive habits takes time and effort, but it can have a significant impact on your overall sense of self-belief and resilience. In this chapter, we will explore how positive habits can be used to build confidence and help you overcome life's challenges.

Setting Habits:

The first step in building confidence through positive habits is to identify what habits you want to build. Start by thinking about areas of your life where you want to improve or feel more confident. This could be related to your physical health, mental well-being, relationships, or personal and professional goals. Once you have identified the areas you want to focus on, you can start setting habits that will help you achieve these goals.

Make the Habit Stick:

Once you have identified the habits you want to build, the next step is to make them stick. This involves being consistent with your habits and making them a part of your daily routine. To do this, try breaking down your habit into smaller, manageable steps that can be completed consistently each day. It can also be helpful to use tools such as reminders, calendars, or habit trackers to help you stay on track.

Embrace the Process:

Building new habits takes time and effort, and it's important to embrace the process and be patient with yourself. It's also important to be flexible and adaptable, as your habits may need to change as your goals and circumstances change. Don't get discouraged if you experience setbacks or miss a day, simply acknowledge the setback and move forward.

Positive Habits to Build:

There are many positive habits that can be used to build confidence, and the right habits for you will depend on your unique goals and circumstances. Here are some positive habits that can have a significant impact on your overall sense of self-belief and resilience:

Exercise: Regular exercise can help improve physical health, boost mood, and reduce stress and anxiety.

Sleep: Getting enough quality sleep is essential for physical and mental well-being.

Meditation and mindfulness: Practicing meditation and mindfulness can help improve focus, reduce stress, and increase self-awareness.

Gratitude: Practicing gratitude can help improve mood and increase a sense of fulfillment and purpose.

Positive self-talk: Positive self-talk can help reduce negative self-criticism and increase self-confidence.

Surrounding yourself with positive influences: Surrounding yourself with positive and supportive people can have a significant impact on your overall well-being and self-belief.

Building confidence through positive habits is a gradual process, but it can have a significant impact on your overall sense of self-belief and resilience. By consistently working on developing positive habits, you can strengthen your confidence and overcome life's challenges with ease. Remember to be patient with yourself, embrace the process, and be flexible and adaptable as your habits and goals change over time.

⅋

"You have within you right now, everything
you need to deal with whatever the world can
throw at you."

- Brian Tracy

VII

Overcoming Fear of Failure and Rejection

Fear of failure and rejection are two common obstacles that can hold us back from achieving our goals and reaching our full potential. These fears can be rooted in past experiences, or they can be a result of negative self-talk and limiting beliefs. However, by overcoming these fears, we can build self-belief and confidence, and we can open the door to new opportunities and possibilities.

To overcome fear of failure, it is important to cultivate a growth mindset. This involves seeing challenges as opportunities for growth and learning, rather than as threats to your abilities or self-worth. By adopting a growth mindset, you can develop a more resilient and optimistic perspective, and you can be more confident in your ability to handle setbacks and challenges.

It is also important to practice self-compassion and to recognize that failure is a natural part of the learning and growth process. By treating yourself with kindness and understanding, rather than self-criticism, you can be more resilient and confident, even in the face of setbacks and challenges.

To overcome fear of rejection, it is important to focus on your own goals and values, and to recognize that rejection is not a reflection of your self-worth or abilities. Instead, rejection can be seen as a learning opportunity, and as a chance to refine your goals and approach.

In addition, it is important to seek support and connection, and to build a network of supportive friends and family who can provide encouragement and motivation. By surrounding yourself with positive and supportive people, you can be more resilient and confident, even in the face of rejection and adversity.

Overcoming fear of failure and rejection is an important step in building self-belief and confidence. By cultivating a growth mindset, practicing self-compassion, focusing on your own goals and values, seeking support and connection, and surrounding yourself with positive and supportive people, you can develop the resilience and confidence you need to overcome life's challenges and reach your full potential.

"You are never too old to set another goal or
to dream a new dream."

- C.S. Lewis

∞

VIII

Managing Emotions The Importance of Self-Care

Self-care is a critical aspect of building self-belief and confidence, and it plays an important role in managing emotions and overcoming life's challenges. Self-care is about taking care of your physical, emotional, and mental health, and it involves setting aside time for self-reflection, relaxation, and activities that bring you joy and fulfillment.

One of the key benefits of self-care is that it helps to regulate emotions. By taking care of yourself and engaging in activities that promote physical and emotional well-being, you can reduce stress and anxiety, and you can better manage negative emotions such as anger, frustration, and sadness.

Self-care also helps to build resilience, which is the ability to bounce back from adversity and to maintain a positive outlook, even in the face of challenges. By engaging in self-care practices such as exercise, mindfulness, and relaxation, you can develop the mental and emotional strength you need to handle life's challenges and to maintain a sense of peace and well-being, even in the face of stress and adversity.

It is important to find self-care practices that work best for you, and to make self-care a priority in your life. This might involve setting aside time each day for self-reflection and relaxation, engaging in physical activities that promote well-being, or seeking support from friends, family, or mental health professionals.

In addition, it is important to recognize that self-care is not a one-time event, but a lifelong commitment. By making self-care a priority in your life, you can maintain your emotional and physical well-being, and you can build the resilience and confidence you need to overcome life's challenges and to reach your full potential.

Self-care is a critical aspect of building self-belief and confidence, and it is essential for managing emotions and overcoming life's challenges. By making self-care a priority in your life, you can regulate your emotions, build resilience, and maintain a sense of peace and well-being, even in the face of stress and adversity.

"*Success is not final, failure is not fatal: it is the courage to continue that counts.*"

- Winston Churchill

IX

Understanding and Managing Self-Criticism

Self-criticism can be a major obstacle to building self-belief and confidence. It involves negative self-talk, focusing on personal shortcomings and mistakes, and doubting one's abilities and self-worth. It can lead to feelings of shame, low self-esteem, and self-doubt, and it can interfere with personal and professional growth.

It is important to recognize that self-criticism is a learned behavior and it is not an accurate reflection of reality. Often, self-criticism stems from childhood experiences and cultural messages that emphasize perfectionism, competitiveness, and the need to be perfect. Additionally, self-criticism can be fueled by fear of failure, fear of rejection, and a need for approval.

To manage self-criticism, it is important to first become aware of your negative self-talk and to challenge these thoughts with self-compassion and self-kindness. This involves recognizing that self-criticism is not an accurate reflection of reality, and that it is not serving you in a positive way. It also involves treating yourself with the same kindness, compassion, and understanding that you would offer to a friend or loved one.

One effective strategy for managing self-criticism is to engage in positive self-talk, which involves speaking kindly and compassionately to yourself, and focusing on your strengths and achievements. This can help to counteract the negative self-talk and to boost self-esteem and confidence.

Another effective strategy for managing self-criticism is to engage in mindfulness and self-reflection. By taking time each day to reflect on your thoughts, emotions, and experiences, you can become more aware of your self-critical thoughts and you can work to reframe these thoughts in a more positive light.

It is also important to recognize that self-criticism can be a form of self-sabotage, and that it can interfere with personal and professional growth. By recognizing this, and by working to manage self-criticism through positive self-talk, self-compassion, and self-reflection, you can build self-belief and confidence and you can overcome life's challenges.

Self-criticism is a common obstacle to building self-belief and confidence, but it is possible to manage it through self-compassion, positive self-talk, and self-reflection. By recognizing the negative impact of self-criticism and by treating yourself with kindness and compassion, you can build self-esteem, boost confidence, and overcome life's challenges.

"Our greatest fear should not be of failure,
but of succeeding at things in life that don't
really matter."

- Francis Chan

&

X

Developing a Growth Mindset

A growth mindset is a belief in one's ability to grow, learn, and improve through hard work and dedication. It is the opposite of a fixed mindset, which is the belief that one's abilities and traits are set in stone and cannot be changed. Research has shown that people with a growth mindset are more likely to persevere in the face of adversity, embrace challenges as opportunities for growth, and view failures as opportunities for learning and improvement.

To develop a growth mindset, it is important to focus on the process of learning and growth, rather than just the outcome. This means embracing challenges, accepting failures as part of the learning process, and recognizing that progress is not always linear.

Another key component of developing a growth mindset is to cultivate a positive and growth-oriented attitude. This involves reframing negative thoughts and emotions, focusing on the positive aspects of life, and adopting a positive and optimistic outlook.

Additionally, it is important to engage in self-reflection and self-assessment. This means taking time each day to reflect on your thoughts, emotions, and experiences, and to assess your progress and identify areas for growth and improvement.

Finally, to develop a growth mindset, it is important to surround yourself with positive and supportive people who encourage and motivate you. This can include family, friends, co-workers, and mentors.

Developing a growth mindset is an important component of building self-belief and confidence. By focusing on the process of learning and growth, cultivating a positive and growth-oriented attitude, engaging in self-reflection and self-assessment, and surrounding yourself with positive and supportive people, you can build self-esteem, boost confidence, and overcome life's challenges.

*"The only person you are destined to become
is the person you decide to be."*

- Ralph Waldo Emerson

XI

Building Support Systems and Connecting with Others

Building strong and supportive relationships with others is a crucial aspect of developing and maintaining self-belief and confidence. Having a support system of family, friends, and other trusted individuals can provide a source of encouragement, motivation, and accountability, as well as a safe space to share your thoughts, feelings, and experiences.

One way to build a support system is to seek out individuals who share similar values, goals, and interests. This can involve joining clubs, organizations, or groups that align with your interests, as well as attending events, workshops, and conferences related to your field or passion. By connecting with others who share your passions, you can build strong and supportive relationships, exchange ideas and information, and grow both personally and professionally.

Another way to build a support system is to seek out mentorship and guidance from experienced individuals who have already navigated the challenges you are facing. This can involve seeking out a coach, mentor, or advisor who can provide guidance, support, and accountability as you work towards your goals.

In addition to building a support system, it is also important to engage in meaningful and positive relationships with others. This can involve volunteering, participating in community events and activities, and taking time to connect with others on a personal level. By building meaningful relationships with others, you can gain a sense of purpose, fulfillment, and belonging, which can boost self-belief and confidence.

Building strong and supportive relationships with others is an important aspect of developing self-belief and confidence. By seeking out individuals who share your passions, seeking mentorship and guidance, and engaging in meaningful and positive relationships, you can build a supportive network that can provide encouragement, motivation, and accountability as you work towards your goals and overcome life's challenges.

"The only way to do great work is to love
what you do."

- Steve Jobs

&

XII

Finding and Pursuing Your Passions

Finding and pursuing your passions is an important aspect of building self-belief and confidence. When you are passionate about something, you are more likely to invest time, effort, and energy into pursuing your goals, which can lead to a greater sense of fulfillment and satisfaction.

The first step to finding your passions is to take time to reflect on your interests, values, and strengths. Ask yourself what activities bring you joy, what causes you are passionate about, and what skills and talents you possess. This can involve trying new activities, exploring new hobbies, and seeking out new experiences.

Once you have identified your passions, the next step is to pursue them with purpose and determination. This can involve setting clear and specific goals, developing a plan of action, and taking consistent and focused action towards your goals. By pursuing your passions with purpose and determination, you can build a sense of purpose, direction, and meaning in your life, which can boost self-belief and confidence.

It is also important to seek out opportunities to develop and grow your passions. This can involve seeking out training and education, volunteering, or seeking out mentorship and guidance from experienced individuals. By developing your passions and skills, you can build greater competence, mastery, and confidence in your abilities, which can further boost self-belief and confidence.

Finding and pursuing your passions is an important aspect of building self-belief and confidence. By taking time to reflect on your interests, values, and strengths, pursuing your passions with purpose and determination, and seeking out opportunities to develop and grow your passions, you can build a sense of purpose, direction, and meaning in your life, and overcome life's challenges with confidence.

"Successful people have a big future in front
of them and a past behind them. But losers
have a past in front of them and a future
behind them."

- Denis Waitley

XIII

Understanding and Managing Perfectionism

Perfectionism can be a major roadblock to building self-belief and confidence. Perfectionism is the belief that anything less than perfect is unacceptable and is often accompanied by an excessive need for control, a fear of failure, and an inability to accept personal limitations.

While a drive for excellence can be a positive attribute, perfectionism can actually have a negative impact on your self-belief and confidence. Perfectionists often set extremely high and unrealistic expectations for themselves, which can lead to feelings of disappointment and frustration when they fall short of their expectations. Additionally, perfectionists often avoid taking risks and trying new things, as they fear making mistakes or falling short of their own expectations.

To overcome perfectionism, it is important to understand the underlying beliefs and thought patterns that drive it. This may involve challenging negative self-talk, such as "I must be perfect" or "I can't make mistakes." It may also involve exploring the root causes of your perfectionism, such as a fear of failure, a need for control, or a desire for approval from others.

Once you have a better understanding of your perfectionism, the next step is to learn to manage it. This can involve setting more realistic and achievable goals, practicing self-compassion, and learning to accept personal limitations. Additionally, it is important to recognize that mistakes and failures are opportunities for growth and learning, rather than evidence of personal inadequacy.

It is also important to develop healthy coping strategies to deal with stress and anxiety. This may involve practicing mindfulness, engaging in physical exercise, or seeking support from friends, family, or a mental health professional.

Perfectionism can be a major roadblock to building self-belief and confidence. To overcome perfectionism, it is important to understand the underlying beliefs and thought patterns that drive it, learn to manage it, and develop healthy coping strategies to deal with stress and anxiety. By learning to accept personal limitations, recognize that mistakes and failures are opportunities for growth and learning, and embracing a growth mindset, you can boost self-belief and confidence, and overcome life's challenges with confidence.

"The best way to predict your future is to create it."

- Abraham Lincoln

XIV

Building Self-Compassion

Self-compassion involves treating oneself with kindness and understanding, especially during difficult times. It is the opposite of self-criticism and is a key component in building self-belief and confidence.

People who have high levels of self-compassion are more likely to have positive self-esteem and are less likely to experience anxiety, depression, and feelings of shame. Moreover, self-compassion has been shown to enhance resilience, improve emotional regulation, and boost motivation.

To build self-compassion, it is important to understand that self-criticism is not an effective motivator and often leads to feelings of shame and self-doubt. Instead, it is better to treat yourself with the same kindness and understanding that you would offer to a friend in a similar situation.

One effective way to build self-compassion is to practice mindfulness. Mindfulness involves paying attention to your thoughts, feelings, and sensations in the present moment without judgment. This can help you to become more aware of your negative self-talk and to shift your focus from self-criticism to self-compassion.

Another effective strategy is to engage in self-care activities, such as exercise, relaxation, and hobbies. This can help to reduce stress and boost feelings of well-being, which in turn can increase self-compassion.

It is also important to surround yourself with supportive people who encourage and celebrate your successes, and who are there for you during tough times. By building a strong support system, you can feel less isolated and better equipped to handle difficult situations.

Self-compassion is a key component in building self-belief and confidence. It involves treating yourself with kindness and understanding, especially during difficult times, and is the opposite of self-criticism. By practicing mindfulness, engaging in self-care activities, and surrounding yourself with supportive people, you can build self-compassion, boost self-esteem, and overcome life's challenges with confidence.

"If you don't design your own life plan,
chances are you'll fall into someone else's
plan. And guess what they have planned for
you? Not much."

- Jim Rohn

XV

Overcoming Life Challenges with Confidence in Self-Belief

Fear of failure and rejection are two common obstacles that can hold us back from achieving our goals and reaching our full potential. These fears can be rooted in past experiences, or they can be a result of negative self-talk and limiting beliefs. However, by overcoming these fears, we can build self-belief and confidence, and we can open the door to new opportunities and possibilities.

To overcome fear of failure, it is important to cultivate a growth mindset. This involves seeing challenges as opportunities for growth and learning, rather than as threats to your abilities or self-worth. By adopting a growth mindset, you can develop a more resilient and optimistic perspective, and you can be more confident in your ability to handle setbacks and challenges.

It is also important to practice self-compassion and to recognize that failure is a natural part of the learning and growth process. By treating yourself with kindness and understanding, rather than self-criticism, you can be more resilient and confident, even in the face of setbacks and challenges.

To overcome fear of rejection, it is important to focus on your own goals and values, and to recognize that rejection is not a reflection of your self-worth or abilities. Instead, rejection can be seen as a learning opportunity, and as a chance to refine your goals and approach.

In addition, it is important to seek support and connection, and to build a network of supportive friends and family who can provide encouragement and motivation. By surrounding yourself with positive and supportive people, you can be more resilient and confident, even in the face of rejection and adversity.

Overcoming fear of failure and rejection is an important step in building self-belief and confidence. By cultivating a growth mindset, practicing self-compassion, focusing on your own goals and values, seeking support and connection, and surrounding yourself with positive and supportive people, you can develop the resilience and confidence you need to overcome life's challenges and reach your full potential.

"You miss 100% of the shots you don't take."

- Wayne Gretzky

৪৩

Other Books Of The Author

1. The Moments When I Met God
2. Kashiyile Theertha Pathangal
3. Guru Gyan Vani
4. Abhiprerak Gita
5. Assi Se Jain Ghat Tak
6. Hopelessness Of Arjuna
7. The Soul And It's True Nature
8. Sense Of Action (Karma)
9. Action Through Wisdom
10. Action Through Wisdom
11. Theory And Practical Of Every Action
12. Logical Understanding Of The Supreme
13. The Imperishable Supreme
14. Yatra Nishadraj Se Hanuman Ghat Tak
15. Yatra Karnatak Ghat Se Raja Ghat Tak
16. Yatra Pandey Ghat Se Prayagraj Ghat Tak
17. Yatra Ranjendra Prasad Ghat Se Dattatreya Ghat Tak
18. Yaatrasindhiya Ghat Se Gwaliar Ghat Tak
19. Yatra Mangala Gauri Ghat Se Hanuman Gadhi Ghat Tak
20. Yatra Gaay Ghat Se Nishad Ghat Tak
21. Maa Ganga, Ghaten Evm Utsav
22. Ganga Arti Dev Deepavali Evam Any Utsav
23. Potentials Of Digitalized India
24. Vedic Consciousness
25. A Brief Introduction To Vedic Science
26. Kashi Ke Barah Jyotirling
27. Impact Of Motivation
28. Let's Have A Milky Way Journey
29. Color Therapy In A Nutshell

30. Rigveda In A Nutshell
31. Yajurveda In A Nutshell
32. Samveda In A Nutshell
33. Atharva Veda In A Nutshell
34. Ayushman Bhava - Ayurveda
35. Srimad Bhagavad Gita And Upanishad Connection
36. Srimad Bhagavad Gita - An Attempt To Summarize Each Chapter.
37. Facts And Impact Of Nakshatra
38. Astro Gems - Navaratna
39. Ekadashi - A Concise Overview
40. A Concise View Of Hanuman Chalisa
41. Inspirational Gita
42. Nakshatraranyam
43. Summary Of 18 Mahapuranas
44. Synopsis Of 18 Upa Puranas
45. Rigvediya Upanishads
46. Shukla Yajurvediya Upanishads
47. Krishna Yajurvediya Upanishads
48. Samavediya Upanishads
49. Atharvavediya Upanishads
50. The Seven Great Sages
51. From Rocket Scientist To President Dr. Apj Abdul Kalam
52. The Visionary's Voice - Quotes Of Dr. Apj Abdul Kalam
53. The Wisdom Of Swami Vivekananda: Insights And Inspiration From A Legendary Spiritual Teacher
54. Ayurvedic Remedies From The Garden
55. Sages And Seers
56. Rising Strong – Motivational Stories Of Women
57. Beyond Flames -Mystery Stories Of Funeral Ghat Manikarnika
58. The Origins Of Tulsi: A Look At The Mythological Roots Of The Plant"

59. The Holistic Cow: A Look At The Physical, Spiritual, And Cultural Importance Of Cows In India
60. Arts Of Healing
61. Exploring The Divine
62. Understanding Five Elements
63. The Etymology Of Ram
64. Symbols Of India
65. Voice Of Change (About Speeches Of Great Men)
66. She Speaks (About Speeches Of Great Women)
67. Patriotism On Celluloid – Brief About Patriotic Films
68. The Music Of Motivation: A Brief Guide To Inspirational Film Songs
69. Unlocking The Secrets of The Dashopanishads
70. A Cultural Mosaic
71. Ancient Traditions, Modern Minds
72. Ecos Of Ancient Wisdom
73. Beneath The Surface
74. From Temples To Ashrams
75. Sages Of The Subcontinent
76. The Art Of Healling (Ayurveda, Yoga & Naturopathy)
77. Indian Kitchen
78. The Festivals Of India
79. The Indian Epics Retold
80. The Power Of Mantras
81. The Indian River Ganges
82. The Indian Architecture
83. Rites Of Passage
84. The Indian Silk Road
85. The Indian Literature
86. The Indian Villages
87. The Indian Folks & Crafts
88. The Way Of Buddha
89. The Ramayan Of Tulsidas

90. Astrological Remedies
91. The Secret Power Of Motivation
92. Secret Of Developing Your Inner Strength
93. The Secret Path To Motivation
94. The Art And Secret Of Positive Thinking
95. The Secrets Of Practicing Ethical Living
96. Indian Art And Painting
97. The Indian Herbalism
98. Bharatanatyam To Kathak
99. Exploring India's Astrological Remedies
100. The Indian Festival Of Flowers
101. Indian Handicrafts
102. The Splashes Of Joy – India's Colour Festival
103. The Indian Science Of Astrology
104. The Indian Mythology
105. Path To Enlightenment
106. The Indian Spirituality For Children
107. Aromas Of India
108. The Secrets Of Healthy Relationships
109. Ancestral Ties
110. The Indian Street Food
111. Discovering America
112. The Indian Textile
113. Listening To Motivational Speeches
114. Taste Of India
115. A Cultural Journey Through Indian Nuptials
116. Motivational Quote For Change
117. Secret Strategies For Making Money
118. Secrets To Cultivate A Positive Mindset
119. A Tapestry Of Cultures: Exploring India From Kashmir To Kanyakumari
120. Achieving Your Dreams With Resilience: Secret Strategies For Overcoming Obstacles

121. Innovative Startups - 25 Startup Ideas To Spark Your Business Creativity
122. Export Management: Strategies For Global Success
123. Exporting From India - A Step By Step Guide
124. Finance Fundamentals: Mastering Financial Management For Business Success
125. Global Growth Strategies For International Business Development
126. Marketing Mastery: Unlocking The Secrets Of Modern Marketing
127. Operations Mastery: Managing The Flow Of Value In Business
128. Strategic Business Management: Navigating The Modern Business Landscape
129. Human Resource Management Strategies For Building And Managing A High Performance Team
130. The Indian Landscapes And Nature: An Exploration Of India's Natural Beauty And Diversity
131. The Indian Street Performances: A Cultural Exploration Of India's Street Performances
132. Affirming Your Self-Worth: Strategies For Achieving Emotional Wellbeing
133. Cultivating Self-Discipline: Secrets Methods For Achieving Your Goals
134. Embracing Change: Strategies For Adapting To Life's Challenges
135. Embracing Your Uniqueness: Secret Strategies For Living An Authentic Life
136. Finding Motivation In Despondency: Coping With Difficult Times
137. Embracing Change
138. Learning To Love Yourself
139. Managing Time For Yourself

140. Unlock The Keys To Self-Motivation
141. Secret To Boost Confidence
142. Unlocking Your Potential: A Path To Inner-Strength & Success
143. Secrets To Develop Authentic Relationship
144. Secrets To Build A Successful Career
145. Secrets To Live With Gratitude
146. Secrets To Create A Life Of Abundance
147. Secrets To Cultivate Self-Awareness
148. The Power Of Helping Hands
149. Finding Your Passion
150. The Indian Mythical Creatures
151. The Indian Women Saints
152. The Wisdom Of The Saints
153. "The Indian Royalty: A Cultural And Historical Exploration Of India's Maharajas And Their Kingdom"
154. The Mystic Land: A Cultural And Spiritual Exploration Of India"
155. India's Spiritual Legacy – Discovering The Cultural And Religious Significance Of Bhakti Yoga.
156. The Indian Folktales: An Exploration Of India's Oral Folklore Traditions
157. Steeping In History: A Look At India's Iconic Tea Culture
158. The Indian Way Of Life: An Exploration Of The Philosophy And Practices Of Indian Culture
159. From Silence To Sound: A Cultural And Historical Study Of Indian Cinema
160. Chronicles Of Indian Style: Tracing The Transformations Of Traditional And Contemporary Fashion
161. Decorating India: A Journey Through The Traditions And Transformations Of Home Design
162. Adornments Of India: A Journey Through The History

And Artistry Behind Indian Jewelry

163. The Indian Royal Kitchens: A Gastronomic Journey Through The Kitchens Of India's Maharajas
164. The Indian Sports: An Insight Into The History And Significance Of Indian Traditional Sports
165. The Indian Traditional Games: A Study Of The Significance And Evolution Of Indian Traditional Games
166. Secrets To Make Positive Choices: Strategies For Achieving Your Goals
167. Secrets To Motivate Yourself For Success Strategies For Reaching Your Goals
168. Secrets To Overcome Adversity: Strategies For Coping With Difficult Times
169. Secrets to Reach Your Goals with Positivity: Strategies for Achieving Your Dreams
170. The Creative Mind: An Exploration of the Secrets to Unleash Your Creativity
171. The Power of Positive Habits: Building Your Life on a Foundation of Success
172. The Secret and Power of Self-Belief: Overcoming Life Challenges with Confidence

CONTACT

DR. JAGADEESH PILLAI

MBA & PhD in Vedic Science

Four Times Guinness World Record Holder

Winner of Mahatma Gandhi Vishwa Shanti Puraskar and
Global Peace Ambassador

Gemology, Astro & Vastu Consultant - Spiritual Counselor

Consultant for designing World Record Ideas

Efficient Tarot Card Reader

9839093003

myrichindia@gmail.com

drjagadeeshpillai@facebook

drjagadeeshpillai@instagram
jagadeeshpillai@youtube

www. JAGADEESHPILLAI.com

|| LOKAHA SAMASTHAHA SUKHINO BHAVANTU ||